ADA-4435
42689996

J
791.84
Sherman

Sherman, Josepha.
Steer wrestling

$21.36

MAR 13 2003

Y0-AIQ-993

OLATHE PUBLIC LIBRARY
201 EAST PARK
OLATHE, KANSAS 66061

Rodeo
★ ★ ★

Steer Wrestling

Josepha Sherman

Heinemann Library
Chicago, Illinois

✪ ✪ ✪

© 2000 Reed Educational & Professional Publishing
Published by Heinemann Library,
an imprint of Reed Educational & Professional Publishing,
100 N. LaSalle, Suite 1010
Chicago, IL 60602
Customer Service 888-454-2279

All rights reserved. No part of this publication may be reproduced or transmitted in any form or by any means, electronic or mechanical, including photocopying, recording, taping, or any information storage and retrieval system, without permission in writing from the publisher.

Designed by Lisa Buckley
Printed in Hong Kong

04 03 02 01 00
10 9 8 7 6 5 4 3 2 1

Library of Congress Cataloging-in-Publication Data
Sherman, Josepha.
    Steer wrestling / Josepha Sherman.
       p. cm. – (Rodeo)
    Includes bibliographical references (p.) and index.
    Summary: Explores the origins and development of steer wrestling as a rodeo event, discussing the rules, the training for wrestling and roping steers, the animals involved, the judging of the events, and stars in wrestling and roping.
    ISBN 1-57572-507-X (library binding)
    1. Steer wrestling—Juvenile literature. 2. Steer roping—Juvenile literature. [1. Steer wrestling. 2. Steer roping. 3. Rodeos.] I. Title.
GV1834.45.S73 S54 2000
791.8'4—dc21   99-048965

Acknowledgments
The author and publishers are grateful to the following for permission to reproduce copyright material:
George F. Mobley/National Geographic, p. 4; Steve Bly, pp. 5, 9, 10, 11, 12, 15; The Granger Collection, p. 6; Corbis-Bettmann, p. 7; Jack Upton, pp. 8, 13, 24, 28; Dudley Barker, pp. 14, 19; William A. Allard/National Geographic, p. 16; Dan Hubbell, pp. 17, 26; National Cowboy Hall of Fame, pp. 18, 27; Erwin C. "Bud" Nielsen/Images International, pp. 20, 21, 22, 23; Joel Sartore/National Geographic, p. 25.

Cover photograph: Dudley Barker

Special thanks to Dan Sullivan of the Calgary Stampede for his comments in the preparation of this book.

Every effort has been made to contact copyright holders of any material reproduced in this book. Any omissions will be rectified in subsequent printings if notice is given to the publisher.

Some words are shown in bold, like this.
You can find out what they mean by looking in the glossary.

Contents

What Is Steer Wrestling? 4

How Steer Wrestling Began. 6

Steer Wrestling Rules 8

The Steer Wrestler 10

The Steers 12

The Horses 14

Judging Steer Wrestling 16

Steer Wrestling Stars 18

Steer Roping 20

Judging Steer Roping 22

Training for Steer Roping 24

Steer Roping Stars. 26

Associations, Museums, and Rodeos 28

Glossary. *30*

More Books to Read *31*

Index. *32*

What Is Steer Wrestling?

Steer wrestling is usually the fastest event at a rodeo.

As the rodeo crowd in the grandstand holds its breath, a **steer**, three or four times larger than any calf and weighing that much more, comes thundering out of a narrow **chute** into the arena. The crowd cheers as barely a moment later a strong-looking cowboy on horseback charges out of a second chute. A second rider cuts in on the steer's left side, keeping the steer from darting sideways.

Now the first cowboy's horse closes in on the steer, almost brushing its side. The cowboy leaps off and grabs the steer by its horns. As his horse races out of the way, the cowboy digs in his heels, sending dirt flying. He pulls backward with all his might to slow down the steer. Then, with strength and skill that makes the crowd gasp, the cowboy wrestles the steer to the ground.

This is the sport of steer wrestling—one cowboy trying to win against a steer that weighs three times as much as he does.

This steer wrestler is just about to grab the steer.

How Steer Wrestling Began

Steer wrestling is one of the few rodeo events that isn't based on ranch work. It is the rodeo creation of a man named Bill Pickett.

Bill Pickett, an African-American cowboy born in the late 1800s, was the thirteenth child of former slaves. He grew up in Texas surrounded by cowboy life. When he was fifteen, Pickett became a cowboy. He might have gone right on being a **ranch hand** if he hadn't discovered a new stunt. It was Bill Pickett who first jumped off a horse, caught a full-grown **steer** by the horns, and wrestled it down.

Bill Pickett was the first steer wrestler.

A steer wrestler has to catch an animal that may be moving as fast as 30 miles (48 kilometers) per hour.

People found this stunt amazing. Soon Pickett was touring with a Wild West Show, which was a combination of circus and traveling rodeo. He showed off his new sport of steer wrestling across North and South America and Europe.

One of Pickett's techniques to control a steer was the same way a bulldog controls its catch. Pickett would wrestle the steer to the ground and then bite its lip. He would hang on this way to keep the steer from trying to get up. By 1910, this method was known as **bulldogging**. Nowadays, a cowboy doesn't bite the steer, but steer wrestling is sometimes still called bulldogging.

Steer Wrestling Rules

In steer wrestling, the **steer** is released from a **chute** into the arena. When the running steer leaves the chute, a count begins so that the steer gets a head start. A **barrier** of two lengths of rope connected by a very thin piece of string is stretched in front of a horse and cowboy. If they begin to chase the steer too early, the horse runs through the rope and breaks the thin string connecting the two ropes. This causes a small flag to raise, alerting the judges that the barrier has been broken, and the cowboy picks up a ten-second penalty.

Once the steer gets its proper head start, the rope barrier goes **slack.** This starts the horse and rider and the event timer.

As the steer wrestler grabs the steer, he digs in his heels to stop it.

The cowboy's horse is trained to get as close to the steer's side as possible. A second rider, called the **hazer**, also pursues the steer. He and his horse force the steer to run in a straight line between the two riders.

When the steer wrestler's horse runs even with the steer, the cowboy slides off and catches the steer's horns. If he does this correctly, the steer's right horn slips neatly into the crook of his right elbow. Sometimes, though, the horn runs up the cowboy's sleeve, ruining his shirt.

The cowboy slows down the steer by digging his heels into the dirt. He has to either stop or turn the steer, or be disqualified. Then the cowboy has to flip the steer onto its side with all four legs pointing in the same direction. A top contestant can do all of this, start to finish, in less than five seconds.

The Steer Wrestler

Steer wrestling is often called the big man's event, and for a very good reason. It takes size and strength, as well as skill, to wrestle a **steer** to the ground. In fact, a steer wrestler is usually muscular and weighs more than 200 pounds (91 kilograms).

But even with his big size, a steer wrestler is going to find himself fighting against the odds. The average steer outweighs a steer wrestler by at least two times and maybe even more. What's more, the running steer is a moving force. It takes a lot of strength to slow the steer down before the cowboy can begin to wrestle it.

By pulling the steer's head toward his body, the steer wrestler can flip an animal over on its side.

This wrestler seems to be having trouble getting the steer to fall.

A good steer wrestler also needs to be a skilled horseman and have expert timing. The steer and the cowboy's horse move at about 35 miles (56 kilometers) per hour when the cowboy leaps from the horse to catch the steer.

The steer wrestling cowboy also needs a good understanding of the principle of leverage. This is basically the idea of moving any object, no matter how big or heavy, by knowing just where to apply force. The principle of leverage makes it possible to raise a car with a jack so that a flat tire can be changed. And leverage is how a 200-pound (91 kilogram) man can throw a 500-pound (227 kilogram) steer.

The Steers

A cowboy and his horse keep a watchful eye on the cattle herd.

Steers, also called doggies in rodeos, are young, full-grown cattle. They are males who cannot have offspring. In the ranch business, steers are usually raised just for meat. In fact, most of the steaks and hamburger in supermarkets comes from steers. In the rodeo world, however, steers are competitors.

There are rules covering rodeo steers. One rule is that a rodeo steer must weigh over 500 pounds (227 kilograms). Another rule is that no one may deliberately cause injury to a steer. Biting a steer's lip to hold it, as was done in the early days of the sport, is no longer allowed. Nor can a steer wrestler put his fingers in the eyes, nose, or mouth of the steer.

Rodeo steers aren't trained in any way. But most animals, including steers, will run if they are suddenly released from a narrow **chute**. Steers are used in rodeos because they are larger and stronger than calves. This gives cowboys more of a challenge. Steers are also used because they are far less dangerous than bulls. No cowboy wants to try throwing a bull! And mean steers are quickly removed from rodeo competition.

A rodeo steer doesn't have to be of any particular breed. Most of them are just cattle that are willing and able to do one thing—run.

A good rodeo steer will be roped or wrestled many times in its career.

The Horses

Part of having horse sense is knowing to get out of the way.

A good steer wrestler's horse doesn't have to be of any special breed. Many of them, though, are likely to be **American quarter horses**, since this is the breed said to have the most cow sense. Cow sense is the ability and desire to herd cattle. Quarter horses are fast enough to keep up with a **steer**, and they are agile enough to get out of the way quickly.

A good rodeo horse isn't scared of the steer. But it also isn't going to try to herd the animal, either! The horse is trained to run as close as possible to the steer without actually bumping it or driving it away. Once the steer wrestler jumps off, the horse's job is to get out of the way as swiftly as possible. The horse moves away when the weight of the rider leaves its back. The motion of the cowboy actually pushes the horse away.

The **hazer's** horse has a somewhat similar job. It must keep running parallel to the steer and never bump into it. This horse must keep the steer going in a straight line and never let it dart in or out. This maneuvering helps the steer wrestler get a good jump onto the steer.

The hazer and his horse keep the steer running in a straight line.

Judging Steer Wrestling

Judges in the steer wrestling event look for several things. They want to see the fastest possible time. Winning **steer** wrestlers usually have times between five and eight seconds.

Judges also look for mistakes or illegal moves. Sometimes the steer wrestler's timing is a little off. Instead of landing so he can neatly grab the steer's horns, he might do a **Houlihan**. This means he lands on the steer's head with such force that the steer falls down. The steer wrestler has to let the steer get back to its feet before he can wrestle it the correct way.

Now that the steer is down, the judges will be looking to see that its legs are all pointing in the same direction.

Leaping off your horse and missing the steer is embarrassing—but sometimes it happens!

Sometimes the steer doesn't fall the right way. It ends up in a **dog fall** instead, with its head pointing away from its legs. The steer wrestler has to either straighten out the steer's head, or throw the steer all over again.

Another mistake that can happen is for a steer wrestler to land with his feet too far apart. Then he can't get enough leverage. The steer can fight him, doing a **rubber neck**. This means the cowboy is bending the steer's neck, but the steer isn't falling.

Steer Wrestling Stars

Fox Hastings

Bynum, Whatley, Melton, and Denton

Steer wrestlers Jim Bynum, Todd Whatley, Gene Melton, and Carl Denton all share one record in common. They all tied the steer wrestling world record of 2.4 seconds: Bynum and Whatley in 1955, and Melton and Denton in 1976. This record was set at rodeos after the rule about barriers was in place.

Oral Zumwalt

Oral Zumwalt set the world's fastest steer wrestling time of 2.2 seconds. However, this was in the 1930s before there were time penalties for riders who didn't wait for the **barrier** to drop.

Fox Hastings

Fox Hastings was one of the few women to try and succeed at steer wrestling. She started her rodeo career at the age of fourteen, when she rode bucking horses and did trick riding. She made her steer wrestling debut in 1924.

Homer Pettigrew

Homer Pettigrew holds the world record for the most steer wrestling world championships. He won six championships in the 1940s. He also holds the world record for the most consecutive steer wrestling championships. He won those in 1942, 1943, 1944, and 1945.

Mike Smith

Mike Smith set a new record for the most money won by a steer wrestler in one year. His prize money in 1998 totaled $161,862.

Mike Smith's work will not be done until the steer falls on its side.

Steer Roping

A steer roper can only catch a steer by the horns.

Steer roping is done by working cowboys and is one of the oldest rodeo events. It dates back to the days before enclosed arenas and grandstands. Steer roping needs more space than other rodeo events, and there is more chance of injury to the **steer**. For these reasons, steer roping is held only at a few rodeos, such as the National Steer Roping Finals held every November in Guthrie, Oklahoma.

Steer roping is similar to **calf roping,** with one major difference. Instead of a calf that weighs about 200 pounds (91 kilograms), the cowboy ropes and ties a steer that is several times the size of a calf and weighs over 500 pounds (227 kilograms).

A steer roper ropes the steer around the horns, and takes a **dally** with the rope around his saddle **horn**. Then he lays **slack** rope over the steer's flank and spurs his horse to move quickly to the left. This jerks the rope and the steer falls to the ground. This take down is called "jerk down" roping or a "jerk back" because of the force needed to get a heavy steer off its feet.

While the roper's horse holds the rope taut, the roper jumps off his horse, catches three of the steer's four legs, and ties them with his **piggin' string**. Time is marked when the contestant throws his hands into the air.

The cowboy jumps from his horse to tie the steer's legs.

Judging Steer Roping

What do judges look for in the steer roping event? They want to see the **steer** roped and tied in the fastest possible time. Top contestants win with times between twelve to fifteen seconds.

Judges also watch that only legal moves are made. There is only one legal way to rope a steer. It must be roped by the horns. For the steer's sake, these horns are protected and strengthened by horn wraps. If the steer roper misses his first try, he is allowed a second chance. But the extra time a second try takes usually keeps a cowboy from winning.

This cowboy has caught the whole head—not a legal catch.

A steer may have the wind knocked out of it in the jerk down.

Judges also watch for the right jerk down. The **slack** rope should be over the steer's right flank and the rider and horse should move swiftly to the left.

Once the steer is thrown, judges watch as the cowboy, leaping from his horse, ties the steer's legs. He must use the proper hooey, or **half-hitch**, knot. Once tied, the steer must remain tied for six seconds, or there's no score for the steer roper.

As in other timed rodeo events, a steer roper who breaks the start **barrier** gets a ten-second penalty.

Training for Steer Roping

How does a cowboy become a steer roper? He might begin his rodeo career as a child. There are several roping events for very young children. The simplest event gives a child under five a chance to rope a dummy **steer** or calf head. The youngster doesn't need to do this from horseback, although some very young children might be steadier in the saddle than they are on their own feet.

There are also schools that teach steer roping, just as there are schools for all other rodeo events. The advantages of a school are that a cowboy learns from doing, and he can get advice from professionals.

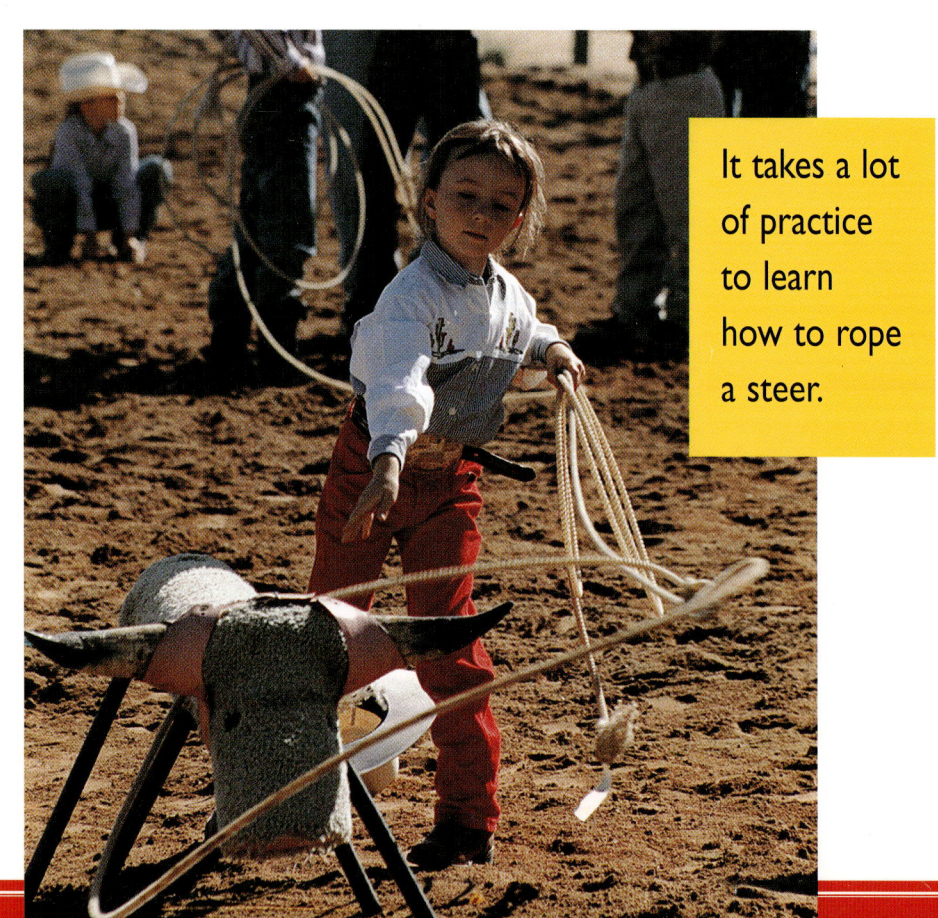

It takes a lot of practice to learn how to rope a steer.

Children younger than five can learn to rope a dummy steer.

A cowboy who wants to be a steer roper usually begins by roping dummy steers. Once he has mastered roping skills and matched them with his riding skills, he's ready to try roping and tying live steers. Rodeo steer roping takes precise timing, expert horsemanship, speed, strength, and accuracy.

Steer Roping Stars

Guy Allen

Guy Allen is one of the top **steer** ropers and possibly one of the best ropers since the sport began. Allen has won an amazing thirteen steer roping championships. He also holds the world record for the most consecutive steer roping championships. From 1991 to 1998, he won eight championships. In addition, Allen set the record in 1996 for the fastest steer roping time of 8.1 seconds. He also won the most money for steer roping in one year. In 1998, his prize money totaled $99,132.

Guy Allen has won more than $900,000 as a steer roper.

Ote Berry

Ote Berry earned four world championships in steer roping. In 1998 he was inducted into the ProRodeo Hall of Fame.

Mabel Strickland

Mabel Strickland was one of the few women steer ropers. She started in rodeos at the age of thirteen and performed for twenty-five years. Strickland was inducted into the ProRodeo Hall of Fame, the Pendleton Round-Up Hall of Fame, and the National Cowgirl Hall of Fame.

Arnold Felts

Arnold Felts was the World Champion Steer Roper in 1981. He was also the top money-earner that year. In addition, he is a four-time winner of the National Steer Roping Finals held in Guthrie, Oklahoma.

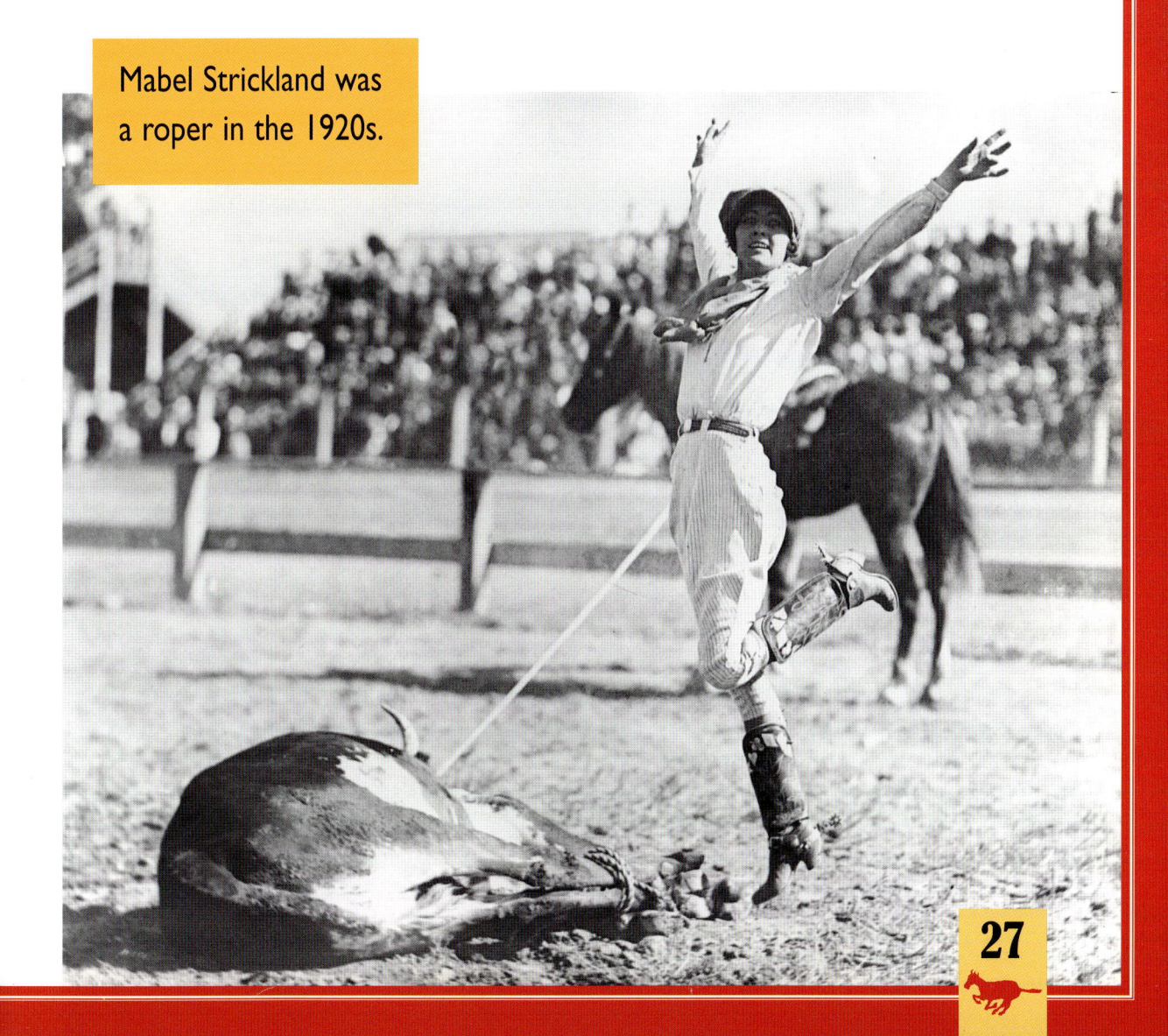

Mabel Strickland was a roper in the 1920s.

Associations, Museums, and Rodeos

Associations:

American Junior Rodeo Association
6029 Loop 306 S.
San Angelo, Tex. 76905
(915) 2572

Candian Professional Rodeo Association
223 2116 27th Avenue, NE
Calgary, Alberta,
Canada T2E 7A6
(403) 250-7440

Professional Rodeo Cowboys Association
101 ProRodeo Drive
Colorado Springs, Colo. 80919
(800) 763-3648

Women's Professional Rodeo Association
1235 Lake Plaza Drive, Suite 134
Colorado Springs, Colo. 80906
(719) 576-0900

Museums:

National Cowboy Hall of Fame
1700 NE 63rd Street
Oklahoma City, Okla. 73111
(405) 478-2250

National Cowgirl Museum and
Hall of Fame
111 West 4th Street
Fort Worth, Tex. 76102
(817) 336-4475
Fax (817) 336-2470

The ProRodeo Hall of Fame
and Museum of the American
Cowboy
Exit 147 - I-25
Colorado Springs, Colo. 80919
(719) 528-4764

Rodeos:

While almost all rodeos include **steer** wrestling, here are a few that also feature steer roping.

Cheyenne Frontier Days
P.O. Box 2477
Cheyenne, Wyo. 82003
(800) 227-6336

Dodge City Roundup
P.O. Box 503
Dodge City, Kans. 67801
(516) 225-2244

Lea County Fair and Rodeo
101 South Commercial Street
Lovington, N.Mex. 88260
(505) 396-5344

Glossary

American quarter horse   breed of horse most often used in ranch work and rodeo events, such as roping and steer wrestling

barrier   rope stretched in front of the contestant's horse that should not be broken or the rider gets a penalty

bulldogging   another name for steer wrestling that came from throwing a steer and biting it on the lip

calf roping   timed rodeo event in which a cowboy must lasso a running calf and keep it tied for six seconds

chute   narrow holding pen that opens into the arena

dally   looping the end of a rope around the saddle horn to secure it

dog fall   in steer wrestling, an illegal fall in which the steer lands with its head pointing away from its legs

half-hitch   type of knot used in calf and steer roping to tie the calf or steer's legs; also called a hooey

hazer   in steer wrestling, the rider whose job it is to keep the steer running in a straight line

horn   front part of a western saddle, that curves up to hold the end of a rope

Houlihan   in steer wrestling, an illegal move of landing on the steer's head with such force that the steer falls

piggin' string   in roping, the soft, six-foot (two meter) rope used to tie a calf or steer's legs

ranch hand   working cowboy on a ranch

rubber neck   when a steer caught by a steer wrestler bends its neck but doesn't fall

slack   loose

steer   young adult male cattle that cannot reproduce

More Books to Read

Acton, Avis. *Behind the Chutes at Cheyenne Frontier Days: Your Pocket Guide to Rodeo.* Cheyenne, Wyo.: A B C Publishing, 1991.

Alter, Judith. *Rodeos: The Greatest Show on Dirt.* New York: Franklin Watts, 1996.

Crum, Robert. *Let's Rodeo!: Young Buckaroos & the World's Wildest Sport.* New York: Simon & Schuster Children's, 1998.

Pinkney, Andrea D. *Bill Pickett: Rodeo-Ridin' Cowboy.* San Diego: Harcourt Brace, 1996.

Sanford, William R., and Carl R. Green. *Bill Pickett: African-American Rodeo Star.* Springfield, New Jersey: Enslow Publishers, 1997.

Index

Allen, Guy 26

barrier 8, 23

Berry, Ote 26

bulldogging 7

Bynum, Jim 18

championships 19, 26

children 24

Denton, Carl 18

dummy steer 25

Felts, Arnold 27

Guthrie, Oklahoma 20, 27

Hastings, Fox 18

hazer 9, 15

horses 4, 5, 6, 8, 9, 11, 14, 15, 21, 23

jerk down 21, 23

judging

   steer roping 22, 23

   steer wrestling 16, 17

Melton, Gene 18

National Cowgirl Hall of Fame 27

National Steer Roping Finals 20, 27

Pettigrew, Homer 19

Pickett, Bill 6

prize money 19

ProRodeo Hall of Fame 26, 27, 29

ranch 6, 12

rules 8, 12

schools 24

Smith, Mike 19

steer wrestler 5, 6, 7, 8, 9, 10, 11, 18

Strickland, Mabel 27

Whatley, Todd 18

world records 19

Zumwalt, Oral 18